Favorite Brand Name

GREAT-TASTING
POTATOES

Publications International, Ltd.

Pictured on the front cover: Fresh Vegetable Casserole *(page 64).*
Pictured on the back cover *(clockwise from top left):* Grilled Cajun Potato Wedges *(page 78),* Grilled Steak & Potato Salad *(page 38)* and Farmstand Frittata *(page 86).*

ISBN: 0-7853-2107-1

Manufactured in U.S.A.

8 7 6 5 4 3 2 1

Nutritional Analysis: Nutritional information is given for some of the recipes in this publication. Each analysis is based on the food items in the ingredient list, except ingredients labeled as "optional" or "for garnish." When more than one ingredient choice is listed, the first ingredient is used for analysis. If a range for the amount of an ingredient is given, the nutritional analysis is based on the lowest amount. Foods offered as "serve with" suggestions are not included in the analysis unless otherwise stated.

Microwave Cooking: Microwave ovens vary in wattage. The microwave cooking times given in this publication are approximate. Use the cooking times as guidelines and check for doneness before adding more time.

GREAT-TASTING
POTATOES

GREAT
Beginnings

Potatoes can add a special touch to an appetizer buffet. Surprise your guests with stuffed new potatoes, homemade herbed chips or spicy potato skins.

Cheesy Potato Skins
with Black Beans & Salsa ▶

6 medium potatoes (6 ounces each), baked

¾ cup GUILTLESS GOURMET® Black Bean Dip (mild or spicy)

¾ cup GUILTLESS GOURMET® Nacho Dip (mild or spicy)

¾ cup GUILTLESS GOURMET® Salsa (mild, medium or hot)

¾ cup low fat sour cream
Fresh cilantro sprigs (optional)

Preheat oven to 400°F. Cut baked potatoes in half lengthwise and scoop out potato pulp, leaving ¼-inch pulp attached to skin (avoid breaking skin). (Save potato pulp for another use, such as mashed potatoes.) Place potato skins on large baking sheet, skin sides down; bake 5 minutes.

Fill each potato skin with 1 tablespoon bean dip and 1 tablespoon nacho dip. Return to oven; bake 10 minutes. Remove from oven; let cool 5 minutes. Dollop 1 tablespoon salsa and 1 tablespoon sour cream onto each potato. Garnish with cilantro, if desired. Serve hot.   *Makes 12 servings*

Nutrients per serving *(1 potato skin): Calories: 133, Total Fat: 1 g, Saturated Fat: 0 g, Cholesterol: 5 mg, Sodium: 216 mg, Protein: 4 g, Dietary Fiber: 3 g*

Southern Stuffed New Potatoes with Wisconsin Asiago, Ham and Mushrooms ▼

12 small new red-skinned potatoes (1½ to 2 inches diameter)
2 tablespoons Wisconsin butter, melted
1 teaspoon Wisconsin butter
2 ounces cooked ham, chopped
¼ cup chopped onion
1 teaspoon chopped fresh thyme
½ teaspoon finely chopped garlic
4 ounces button mushrooms, chopped
2½ ounces portobello mushrooms, chopped*

2½ ounces oyster mushrooms, stemmed and chopped*
3 tablespoons whipping cream
½ cup (2 ounces) shredded Wisconsin Asiago cheese
Salt
Black pepper
½ cup (2 ounces) shredded Wisconsin baby Swiss cheese
½ cup (2 ounces) shredded Wisconsin medium white Cheddar cheese
¼ cup chopped fresh parsley

Preheat oven to 400°F. Cut ¼ inch off each end of potatoes; discard ends. Cut potatoes in half crosswise. In large bowl, stir together potatoes and 2 tablespoons melted butter until potatoes are well coated. Place potatoes on parchment-lined 15×10-inch jelly-roll pan. Bake for 30 to 40 minutes or until fork tender. Let cool slightly. Scoop out potato pulp, leaving thin shells. Reserve potato pulp for another use. Set shells aside.

Melt 1 teaspoon butter in large skillet over medium-high heat. Add ham; cook 2 to 5 minutes or just until ham begins to brown, stirring occasionally. Add onion, thyme and garlic; decrease heat to medium-low. Cook and stir 2 to 3 minutes or until onion is tender. Add mushrooms. Cook 5 to 6 minutes or until liquid is evaporated, stirring occasionally. Add whipping cream; cook 1 minute, stirring constantly, or until cream is thickened. Stir in Asiago cheese. Season to taste with salt and pepper.

Remove skillet from heat. Meanwhile, in medium bowl, combine baby Swiss and white Cheddar cheeses; set aside. Fill potato shells with mushroom mixture; sprinkle evenly with Swiss and Cheddar cheese mixture. Cover; refrigerate overnight. To bake, allow potatoes to stand at room temperature for 45 minutes. Preheat oven to 400°F. Bake 12 to 15 minutes or until cheeses are melted and lightly browned. Sprinkle with chopped parsley. *Makes 24 appetizers*

*Substitute 5 ounces button mushrooms for portobello and oyster mushrooms, if desired.

Favorite recipe from **Wisconsin Milk Marketing Board**

Nacho Potato Appetizers

2 Colorado russet variety
   potatoes, cut into ¼-inch
   slices
¼ cup taco sauce
¼ cup roasted red pepper, cut
   into julienne strips
¼ cup pitted black olives, cut into
   wedges

1½ cups (6 ounces) shredded
   Cheddar or Monterey Jack
   cheese
   Cilantro or parsley sprigs
¼ cup sour cream or plain yogurt
½ cup salsa

continued on page 10

Preheat oven to 375°F. Grease shallow baking pan. Arrange potato slices in prepared pan. Brush tops with taco sauce. Bake for 10 minutes or until tender. Top with pepper, olives and cheese. Bake 5 minutes longer or until cheese is melted. Garnish with cilantro. Serve with sour cream and salsa.   *Makes 4 servings*

Green Guacamole Nachos: Combine 1 mashed small ripe avocado, ¼ cup softened pimiento-flavored cream cheese, 2 tablespoons chopped green chilies, 1 teaspoon lime juice and ⅛ teaspoon garlic salt. Substitute avocado mixture for peppers, olives and cheese. Bake and serve as directed above.

Nutrients per serving: Calories: 336, Total Fat: 18 g, Cholesterol: 51 mg, Sodium: 602 mg, Protein: 14 g, Dietary Fiber: 3 g

*Favorite recipe from **Colorado Potato Administrative Committee***

Beef & Potato Empanadas

6 ounces cooked roast beef,
   shredded
½ cup chopped green onion tops
¼ cup finely chopped onion
1 tablespoon canned chopped
   jalapeño pepper
½ teaspoon bottled minced garlic

½ teaspoon salt
½ teaspoon black pepper
2 medium Colorado potatoes,
   cooked, peeled and chopped
¼ cup beef broth
2 frozen puff pastry sheets,
   thawed

To make filling, combine beef, green onions, onion, jalapeño pepper, garlic, salt and black pepper in medium bowl; mix well. Stir in potatoes and enough of the beef broth to moisten and hold mixture together.

Preheat oven to 400°F. Roll out each pastry sheet to 12×12-inch square on lightly floured surface. Cut each square into nine 4-inch squares. Place rounded tablespoonful of filling on each square. Fold over to form triangle; seal edges with fork. Place on baking sheet. Bake about 20 minutes or until golden.   *Makes 18 empanadas*

Nutrients per serving (1 empanada): Calories: 146, Total Fat: 8 g, Cholesterol: 6 mg, Sodium: 213 mg, Protein: 5 g, Dietary Fiber: trace

*Favorite recipe from **Colorado Potato Administrative Committee***

Spicy Lamb & Potato Nests

Potato Nests

    2 unpeeled small Colorado
        potatoes, shredded
    1 egg
    1 tablespoon vegetable oil
    1 tablespoon grated Parmesan
        cheese
    ¼ teaspoon garlic powder
    ¼ teaspoon black pepper
    ¼ cup biscuit mix
        Fine, dry bread crumbs

Lamb Filling

    8 ounces lean ground lamb
    ¼ cup chopped green onion
    1 teaspoon grated fresh ginger
        or ¼ teaspoon dry ginger
    ½ teaspoon ground cumin
    ¼ teaspoon salt
    ¼ teaspoon ground coriander
    ¼ teaspoon ground cinnamon
    ¼ teaspoon ground red pepper
    ¼ cup jalapeño pepper jelly

To prepare Potato Nests, place potatoes in medium bowl. Cover with cold water; let stand 5 minutes. Drain well; pat dry with paper towels. Preheat oven to 400°F. Whisk together egg, oil, cheese, garlic powder and black pepper. Stir in biscuit mix until well blended. Stir in shredded potato. Generously grease 16 muffin cups; sprinkle bottom of each lightly with bread crumbs. Spoon about 1 tablespoon of potato mixture into each cup; make slight indentation in center. Bake 15 minutes. Remove from oven and keep warm.

Meanwhile to prepare Lamb Filling, cook and stir lamb and onion in saucepan over medium-high heat until lamb is no longer pink and onion is tender. Drain well; add ginger, cumin, salt, coriander, cinnamon and red pepper. Cook and stir 1 to 2 minutes until flavors are blended. Add jelly; heat until jelly is melted and lamb mixture is heated through. Spoon lamb mixture by rounded teaspoonfuls onto potato nests. Serve hot.

Makes 16 appetizers

Note: Spicy Lamb & Potato Nests may be made ahead, covered and refrigerated. Just before serving wrap in foil and heat in preheated 350°F oven for 10 minutes.

Nutrients per serving (1 appetizer): Calories: 68, Total Fat: 3 g, Cholesterol: 22 mg, Sodium: 78 mg, Protein: 3 g, Dietary Fiber: trace

*Favorite recipe from **Colorado Potato Administrative Committee***

Herbed Potato Chips ▶

Nonstick olive oil cooking
  spray
2 medium unpeeled red skinned
  potatoes
1 tablespoon olive oil
2 tablespoons minced fresh dill,
  thyme or rosemary *or*
  2 teaspoons dried dill weed,
  thyme or rosemary

¼ teaspoon garlic salt
⅛ teaspoon black pepper
1¼ cups nonfat sour cream

1. Preheat oven to 450°F. Spray large nonstick baking sheets with nonstick cooking spray; set aside.

2. Cut potatoes crosswise into very thin slices, about ¹⁄₁₆ inch thick. Pat dry with paper towels. Arrange potato slices in single layer on prepared baking sheets; coat potatoes with nonstick cooking spray.

3. Bake 10 minutes; turn slices over. Brush with oil. Combine dill, garlic salt and pepper in small bowl; sprinkle evenly onto potato slices. Continue baking 5 to 10 minutes or until potatoes are golden brown. Cool on baking sheets. Serve with sour cream.

Makes about 60 chips

Nutrients per serving *(10 chips, about 3 tablespoons sour cream): Calories: 76 , Total Fat: 2 g, Saturated Fat: trace, Cholesterol: 0 mg, Sodium: 113 mg, Protein: 6 g, Dietary Fiber: trace*

Potato Pancake Appetizers ▶

3 medium Colorado russet
   potatoes peeled and grated
1 egg
2 tablespoons all-purpose flour
1 teaspoon salt
¼ teaspoon black pepper
1 cup grated carrot (1 large)

1½ cups grated zucchini (2 small)
½ cup low-fat sour cream or
   plain yogurt
2 tablespoons finely chopped
   fresh basil
1 tablespoon chopped chives *or*
   1½ teaspoons chili powder

Preheat oven to 425°F. Wrap potatoes in several layers of paper towels; squeeze to remove excess moisture. Beat egg, flour, salt and pepper in large bowl. Add potatoes, carrot and zucchini; mix well. Oil 2 nonstick baking sheets. Place vegetable mixture by heaping spoonfuls onto baking sheets; flatten slightly. Bake 8 to 15 minutes until bottoms are browned. Turn; bake 5 to 10 minutes more. Stir together sour cream and herbs; serve with warm pancakes.
Makes about 24 appetizer pancakes

Nutrients per serving (1 pancake): Calories: 29, Total Fat: 1 g, Cholesterol: 11 mg, Sodium: 96 mg, Protein: 1 g, Dietary Fiber: 1 g

*Favorite recipe from **Colorado Potato Administrative Committee***

Cheesy Potato Skins

2 tablespoons grated Parmesan
   cheese
3 cloves garlic, finely chopped
2 teaspoons dried rosemary
½ teaspoon salt

¼ teaspoon black pepper
4 baking potatoes, baked
2 egg whites, slightly beaten
½ cup (2 ounces) shredded part-
   skim mozzarella cheese

Preheat oven to 400°F. Combine Parmesan cheese, garlic, rosemary, salt and pepper in small bowl. Cut potatoes lengthwise in half. Remove pulp, leaving ¼-inch-thick shells. Reserve pulp for another use. Cut potatoes lengthwise into wedges. Place on baking sheet. Brush with egg whites; sprinkle with Parmesan cheese mixture. Bake 20 minutes. Sprinkle with mozzarella cheese; bake until mozzarella cheese is melted. Serve with salsa, if desired.
Makes 8 servings

Nutrients per serving: Calories: 90, Total Fat: 2 g, Saturated Fat: 1 g, Cholesterol: 5 mg, Sodium: 215 mg, Protein: 5 g, Dietary Fiber: 2 g

Hot & Spicy Ribbon Chips ▲

6 medium unpeeled Colorado
    russet potatoes
1 tablespoon plus 1 teaspoon
    salt, divided
Vegetable oil

1 tablespoon chili powder
1 teaspoon garlic salt
¼ to ½ teaspoon ground red
    pepper

With vegetable peeler, make thin lengthwise potato ribbons. Place in large bowl with
1-quart ice water mixed with 1 tablespoon salt. Heat oil in deep-fat fryer or heavy pan to
365°F. Combine chili powder, remaining 1 teaspoon salt, garlic salt and red pepper; set
aside. Drain potatoes and pat dry with paper towels. Fry potatoes in batches until crisp
and golden brown; remove with slotted spoon to paper towels. Sprinkle with chili
powder mixture. *Makes 8 to 12 servings*

Nutrients per serving (⅛ *of recipe*): *Calories: 91, Total Fat: 4 g, Cholesterol: 0 mg,
Sodium: 343 mg, Protein: 2 g, Dietary Fiber: 1 g*

Favorite recipe from **Colorado Potato Administrative Committee**

Great Beginnings 15

One Potato, Two Potato ▶

2 medium baking potatoes, cut lengthwise into 4 wedges
Nonstick cooking spray
Salt
½ cup unseasoned dry bread crumbs
2 tablespoons grated Parmesan cheese (optional)

1½ teaspoons dried oregano leaves, dill weed, Italian herbs or paprika
Spicy brown or honey mustard, ketchup or reduced-fat sour cream

1. Preheat oven to 425°F. Spray baking sheet with nonstick cooking spray; set aside.

2. Spray cut sides of potatoes generously with cooking spray; sprinkle lightly with salt.

3. Combine bread crumbs, Parmesan cheese and desired herb in shallow dish. Add potatoes; toss lightly until potatoes are generously coated with crumb mixture. Place on prepared baking sheet.

4. Bake potatoes until browned and tender, about 20 minutes. Serve warm as dippers with mustard.

Makes 4 servings

Potato Sweets: Omit Parmesan cheese, herbs and mustard. Substitute sweet potatoes for baking potatoes. Cut and spray potatoes as directed; coat generously with desired amount of cinnamon-sugar. Bake as directed. Serve warm as dippers with peach or pineapple preserves or honey mustard.

Nutrients per serving: Calories: 165, Total Fat: 1 g, Saturated Fat: trace, Cholesterol: 0 mg, Sodium: 124 mg, Protein: 4 g, Dietary Fiber: 3 g

Great Beginnings

COMFORTING
Soups & Stews

You'll find everything from ever-popular Cheesy Potato Soup to trendy Spicy African Chick-Pea and Sweet Potato Stew in this splendid collection.

Potato & Cheddar Soup ▶

2 cups red-skinned potatoes, peeled and cut into cubes
3 tablespoons margarine or butter
1 small onion, finely chopped
3 tablespoons all-purpose flour
Ground red pepper

Black pepper
3 cups milk
½ teaspoon salt
1 cup cubed cooked ham
1 cup (4 ounces) shredded Cheddar cheese

Bring 2 cups water to a boil in large saucepan. Add potatoes; simmer until tender. Drain, reserving liquid. Measure 1 cup reserved liquid, adding water if necessary. Melt margarine in same saucepan over medium heat. Add onion; cook and stir until tender but not brown. Stir in flour; season to taste with red and black pepper. Cook 3 to 4 minutes. Gradually add potatoes, reserved liquid, milk and salt to onion mixture; stir well. Add ham. Simmer over low heat 5 minutes, stirring frequently. Remove from heat; cool 5 minutes. Stir in cheese until melted. *Makes 3 to 4 servings*

Chunky Garden Stew ▶

Spicy Hot Sauce (recipe follows)

1 tablespoon olive or canola oil

3 medium Colorado Sangre red potatoes, cut into chunks

1 large carrot, sliced diagonally

1 medium onion, quartered

1 large yellow squash or zucchini, sliced

1 Japanese eggplant *or* ½ regular eggplant, cut into cubes

2 celery stalks, sliced

1 small red or green bell pepper, cut into chunks

1 teaspoon ground cinnamon

1 teaspoon coriander

1 teaspoon turmeric

½ teaspoon ground cumin

½ teaspoon ground cardamom

½ teaspoon salt

2 cans (14½ ounces each) vegetable broth *or* 1½ cups water

1 can (15 ounces) chick-peas, drained

⅔ cup raisins

6 cups hot cooked rice

Prepare Spicy Hot Sauce; set aside. Heat oil in Dutch oven over medium-high heat. Add potatoes and carrot; cook and stir 5 minutes. Add onion, squash, eggplant, celery, bell pepper, spices and salt; cook and stir 3 to 5 minutes. Add broth, chick-peas and raisins; bring to a simmer. Simmer, covered, about 15 minutes or until potatoes are tender. Serve vegetable stew over rice. Serve with Spicy Hot Sauce.   *Makes 5 to 6 servings*

Spicy Hot Sauce

⅓ cup coarsely chopped cilantro

¼ cup water

1 tablespoon olive or canola oil

2 cloves garlic

½ teaspoon salt

½ teaspoon turmeric

¼ to ½ teaspoon ground red pepper

¼ teaspoon sugar

¼ teaspoon ground cumin

¼ teaspoon ground cardamom

¼ teaspoon ground coriander

Combine all ingredients in blender; process until smooth. Adjust flavors to taste.

Makes about ½ cup sauce

Nutrients per serving (¹/₅ *of recipe*): *Calories: 456 g, Total Fat: 7 g, Cholesterol: 0 mg, Sodium: 397 mg, Protein: 15 g, Dietary Fiber: 12 g*

Favorite recipe from **Colorado Potato Administrative Committee**

Idaho® Potato Chili ▲

1 pound Idaho® potatoes, peeled
    and cut into ½-inch cubes
    (about 2½ cups)
1 tablespoon vegetable oil
1 large onion, chopped (about
    1 cup)
1 green bell pepper, diced
    (about 1 cup)
1 clove garlic, minced
8 ounces ground turkey
2 tablespoons chili powder

1 can (28 ounces) whole
    tomatoes, undrained
1 can (16 ounces) kidney beans,
    drained and rinsed
½ teaspoon salt
¼ cup chopped fresh cilantro
¼ cup plain nonfat yogurt *or*
    2 tablespoons low-fat sour
    cream
¼ cup sliced green onions *or*
    chopped tomato

1. Heat oil in large saucepan over medium-high heat. Add onions, pepper and garlic. Cook and stir 5 minutes or until softened.

2. Add turkey. Cook and stir 5 to 6 minutes or until no longer pink, breaking up with spoon.

3. Stir in chili powder. Cook for 1 minute. Add canned tomatoes, potatoes, beans, 1 cup water and salt. Bring to a boil. Reduce heat to low. Simmer, covered, 30 minutes, stirring occasionally.

4. Remove from heat. Stir in cilantro. Top with yogurt and green onions, if desired.

Makes 4 to 6 servings

Nutrients per serving (¹⁄₆ of recipe): Calories: 316, Total Fat: 8 g, Cholesterol: 39 mg, Sodium: 770 mg, Protein: 19 g

Favorite recipe from **Idaho® Potato**

Corn and Potato Chowder

Nonstick cooking spray
1 cup chopped onions
½ cup sliced green bell pepper
½ cup sliced red bell pepper
1 large clove garlic, minced
2 cans (10½ ounces each) reduced-salt chicken broth
1 can (16½ ounces) no-salt-added cream-style corn
1 can (15¼ ounces) no-salt-added whole kernel corn, drained

1 can (16 ounces) whole potatoes, drained and sliced
¼ teaspoon ground cumin
4 dashes hot pepper sauce
¼ to ½ teaspoon black pepper
2 slices bacon, cooked, drained and crumbled
Minced parsley

Spray large saucepan with cooking spray; cook and stir onions, bell peppers and garlic until tender. Stir in broth, corn, potatoes and cumin. Bring to a boil. Reduce heat to medium-low and simmer, uncovered, 15 to 20 minutes. Stir in pepper sauce and black pepper. Spoon into bowls; sprinkle with bacon and parsley.

Makes 4 servings (about 2 cups each)

Favorite recipe from **Canned Food Information Council**

Sweet Potato and Ham Soup ▶

1 tablespoon margarine or
    butter
1 small leek, sliced
1 clove garlic, minced
½ pound ham, cut into ½-inch
    cubes
2 medium sweet potatoes, peeled
    and cut into ¾-inch cubes

4 cups canned chicken broth
½ teaspoon dried thyme leaves,
    crushed
2 ounces fresh spinach, coarsely
    chopped

1. Melt margarine in large saucepan over medium heat. Add leek and garlic. Cook and stir until leek is limp.

2. Add ham, sweet potatoes, broth and thyme to saucepan. Bring to a boil over high heat. Reduce heat to medium-low. Cook 10 minutes or until sweet potatoes are tender.

3. Stir spinach into soup. Simmer, uncovered, 2 minutes or until spinach is wilted. Serve immediately.
Makes 6 servings

Farmer's Cold Tater Soup

2 to 3 Colorado potatoes, peeled
2 large onions, minced
2 leeks, minced (white parts
    only)
4 cups water

1 cup canned chicken broth
1 tablespoon butter, melted
1 tablespoon flour
2 cups hot milk*
    Chopped chives for garnish

Combine potatoes, onions, leeks and water in large saucepan over high heat. Bring to a boil. Reduce heat to medium-low. Simmer 25 minutes or until potatoes are tender. Process vegetables in blender or food processor until smooth; return to saucepan. Add broth. Combine butter and flour until blended. Stir into potato mixture. Bring to a boil. Boil 1 minute. Stir in hot milk. Cool soup to room temperature; refrigerate until cold. Garnish with chopped chives.
Makes 4 to 6 servings

*For a richer soup, replace 1 cup milk with 1 cup half-and-half.

Nutrients per serving *(¼ of recipe): Calories: 216, Total Fat: 6 g, Cholesterol: 17 mg, Sodium: 348 mg, Protein: 8 g, Dietary Fiber: 3 g*

Favorite recipe from **Colorado Potato Administrative Committee**

New England Clam Chowder ▶

24 medium clams
Salt
1 bottle (8 ounces) clam juice
3 medium potatoes, cut into
  ½-inch-thick slices
¼ teaspoon dried thyme leaves,
  crushed
¼ teaspoon ground white pepper

4 slices bacon, cut crosswise into
  ¼-inch-wide strips
1 medium onion, chopped
⅓ cup all-purpose flour
2 cups milk
1 cup half-and-half
Oyster crackers
Fresh thyme for garnish

1. Scrub clams. Soak clams in mixture of ⅓ cup salt to 1 gallon water 20 minutes. Drain water; repeat. Place clams on tray and refrigerate 1 hour to help clams relax. Shuck clams; place clams and their juice in strainer over bowl. Strain clam juice through triple thickness of dampened cheesecloth into 2-cup measure. Coarsely chop clams; set aside.

2. Add bottled clam juice and enough water to clam juice in glass measure to total 2 cups; place clam juice mixture in Dutch oven. Add potatoes, thyme and pepper. Bring to a boil. Reduce heat to low. Simmer 15 minutes or until potatoes are tender, stirring occasionally.

3. Meanwhile, cook bacon in medium skillet over medium heat until almost crisp. Add onion; cook until tender but not brown.

4. Stir flour into bacon mixture. Whisk in milk using wire whisk. Cook until mixture boils and thickens. Add bacon mixture and half-and-half to potato mixture. Add clams; heat until clams are firm. Serve chowder with oyster crackers. Garnish, if desired.

Makes 6 main-dish servings

Spicy African Chick-Pea and Sweet Potato Stew

Spice Paste (recipe follows)
1½ pounds sweet potatoes, peeled and cubed
2 cups canned vegetable broth or water
1 can (16 ounces) chick-peas, drained and rinsed
1 can (14½ ounces) plum tomatoes, undrained and chopped

1½ cups sliced fresh okra *or*
1 package (10 ounces) frozen cut okra, thawed
Yellow Couscous (recipe follows)
Hot pepper sauce
Fresh cilantro for garnish

1. Prepare Spice Paste.

2. Combine sweet potatoes, broth, chick-peas, tomatoes and juice, okra and Spice Paste in large saucepan. Bring to a boil over high heat. Reduce heat to low. Cover and simmer 15 minutes. Uncover; simmer 10 minutes or until vegetables are tender.

3. Meanwhile, prepare Yellow Couscous.

4. Serve stew with couscous and pepper sauce. Garnish, if desired.

Makes 4 servings

Spice Paste

6 cloves garlic, peeled
1 teaspoon coarse salt
2 teaspoons sweet paprika
1½ teaspoons cumin seeds

1 teaspoon cracked black pepper
½ teaspoon ground ginger
½ teaspoon ground allspice
1 tablespoon olive oil

Process garlic and salt in blender or small food processor until garlic is finely chopped. Add remaining spices. Process 15 seconds. While blender is running, pour oil through cover opening; process until mixture forms paste.

Yellow Couscous

1 tablespoon olive oil
5 green onions, sliced
1⅔ cups water
⅛ teaspoon saffron threads *or*
    ½ teaspoon ground turmeric
¼ teaspoon salt
1 cup precooked couscous*

1. Heat oil in medium saucepan over medium heat until hot. Add onions; cook and stir 4 minutes. Add water, saffron and salt. Bring to a boil. Stir in couscous. Remove from heat. Cover; let stand 5 minutes.   *Makes 3 cups*

*Check ingredient label for "precooked semolina."

Cheesy Potato Soup

4 baking potatoes, scrubbed
    (about 1½ pounds)
2 tablespoons butter
1 medium onion, sliced
2 tablespoons all-purpose flour
1 teaspoon beef bouillon
    granules
2 cups water
1 can (12 ounces) evaporated
    milk
1 cup (4 ounces) shredded
    Wisconsin brick cheese
1 teaspoon chopped parsley
¾ teaspoon Worcestershire sauce
¾ teaspoon salt
¾ teaspoon black pepper

Microwave Directions: Pierce potatoes several times with fork. Microwave on paper towel at HIGH 10 to 12 minutes or until potatoes are soft; cool. Place butter and onion in large bowl. Microwave at HIGH 2 minutes or until tender. Stir in flour. Stir in bouillon granules and water until well blended. Microwave at HIGH 2 minutes or until onion mixture is heated. Scoop out potato pulp, leaving it in chunks. Add potato pulp, evaporated milk, cheese, parsley, Worcestershire, salt and pepper to onion mixture. Microwave at HIGH 2½ to 4 minutes or until cheese is melted and soup is hot.

Makes 6 servings

Nutrients per serving: Calories: 308, Total Fat: 14 g, Cholesterol: 45 mg, Sodium: 614 mg, Protein: 12 g

*Favorite recipe from **Wisconsin Milk Marketing Board***

Beef Stew in Red Wine ▶

1½ pounds lean boneless beef round steak, cut into 1-inch cubes

1½ cups dry red wine

2 teaspoons olive oil
Peel of half an orange

2 large cloves garlic, thinly sliced

1 bay leaf

½ teaspoon dried thyme leaves, crushed

⅛ teaspoon black pepper

8 ounces mushrooms, quartered

8 sun-dried tomatoes, quartered

1 can (about 14 ounces) reduced-sodium beef broth

6 small unpeeleed potatoes, scrubbed and cut into wedges

1 cup baby carrots

1 cup pearl onions, skins removed

1 tablespoon cornstarch

2 tablespoons water

1. Combine beef, wine, oil, orange peel, garlic, bay leaf, thyme and pepper in large glass bowl. Refrigerate, covered, at least 2 hours or overnight.

2. Place beef mixture, mushrooms and tomatoes in large nonstick skillet or Dutch oven. Add enough broth to just cover ingredients. Bring to a boil over high heat. Cover; reduce heat to low. Simmer 1 hour. Add potatoes, carrots and onions; cover and cook 20 to 25 minutes or until vegetables are tender. Remove meat and vegetables from skillet with slotted spoon; cover and set aside. Discard orange peel and bay leaf.

3. Combine cornstarch and water until blended. Stir into skillet with sauce. Increase heat to medium; cook, stirring until sauce is slightly thickened. Return meat and vegetables to sauce; cook until heated through. *Makes 6 servings*

Nutrients per serving: Calories: 313 , Total Fat: 6 g, Saturated Fat: 1 g, Cholesterol: 55 mg, Sodium: 304 mg, Protein: 26 g, Dietary Fiber: 3 g

POTATO
Salads Galore

Potato salads aren't just for picnics–they're a hit any time of the year. Dress them up with a touch of pesto, crisp change-of-pace snow peas or sweet Italian sausages and wait for the applause.

Potato & Prosciutto Salad ▶

3 medium Colorado Sangre red
   potatoes, unpeeled
½ pound green beans, trimmed
   and cut into 2½-inch pieces
1 red bell pepper, thinly sliced
1½ cups frozen corn, thawed
6 ounces mozzarella cheese, cut
   into ½-inch cubes
3 ounces thinly sliced prosciutto
   or ham, cut into strips

3 green onions, sliced
⅓ cup olive oil
¼ cup lemon juice
2 tablespoons water
1 to 2 cloves garlic, minced
1 tablespoon chopped fresh
   thyme *or* 1½ teaspoon dried
   thyme leaves
Salt and black pepper

Cook potatoes in boiling water 25 minutes until tender. Drain; cool. Cut into ½-inch-thick slices; cut into quarters. Cook green beans in boiling water until tender. Drain; cool. Combine potatoes, beans, bell pepper, corn, cheese, prosciutto and onions in large bowl. Whisk together oil, lemon juice, water, garlic and thyme. Pour dressing over potato mixture; toss to coat. Season to taste. *Makes 6 to 8 servings*

Nutrients per Serving *(⅛ of recipe): Calories: 237, Total Fat: 12 g, Cholesterol: 17 mg, Sodium: 254 mg, Protein: 11 g, Dietary Fiber: 3 g*

Favorite recipe from **Colorado Potato Administrative Committee**

Salad Niçoise

1 box (9 ounces) BIRDS EYE®
   frozen Cut Green Beans
1 head Boston or green leaf
   lettuce
1 can (16 ounces) whole
   potatoes, drained and cut
   into ¼-inch slices

1 can (6 ounces) tuna packed in
   water, drained
2 tomatoes, cut into wedges
⅓ cup Greek or black olives
⅓ cup Caesar salad dressing

COOK green beans according to package directions. Drain and rinse under cold water to cool; drain well.

ARRANGE lettuce leaves on serving platter. Arrange beans, potatoes, tuna, tomatoes and olives in separate piles on lettuce.

DRIZZLE dressing over salad.
Makes about 4 servings

Prep Time: 10 minutes   **Cook Time:** 5 minutes

Pear and Potato Salad

1 cup BLUE DIAMOND® Blanched
   Slivered Almonds
1 tablespoon olive oil
½ cup mayonnaise
2 cloves garlic, finely chopped
½ teaspoon salt
¼ teaspoon grated fresh ginger
   or ⅛ teaspoon ground
   ginger
¼ teaspoon black pepper
½ cup chopped fresh parsley

½ pound new potatoes, peeled
   and diced
1 pound slightly firm pears,
   peeled, cored, diced and
   tossed with 1 tablespoon
   lemon juice
1 medium red bell pepper, diced
½ cup thinly sliced green onions
   (including white and green
   parts)

Sauté almonds in oil until golden; set aside. Combine mayonnaise, garlic, salt, ginger and black pepper in medium bowl. Fold in parsley; set aside. Cook potatoes in salted, boiling water until just tender. (Do not overcook.) Drain; while still warm, combine with dressing. Cool to room temperature. Fold in pears, bell pepper and green onions. Chill. Just before serving, fold in almonds.
Makes 4 to 6 servings

Santa Fe Potato Salad ▼

5 medium white potatoes
½ cup vegetable oil
¼ cup red wine vinegar
1 package (1.0 ounce) LAWRYS®
 Taco Spices & Seasonings
1 can (7 ounces) whole kernel
 corn, drained
⅔ cup sliced celery

⅔ cup shredded carrot
⅔ cup chopped red or green bell
 pepper
2 cans (2.25 ounces each) sliced
 ripe olives, drained
½ cup chopped red onion
2 tomatoes, wedged and halved

In large saucepan, cook potatoes in boiling water until tender, about 30 minutes;
drain. Let cool slightly; cube. In small bowl, combine oil, vinegar and Taco Spices &
Seasonings; blend well. Add to warm potatoes; toss gently to coat. Cover; refrigerate at
least 1 hour. Gently fold in remaining ingredients. Chill thoroughly.

Makes 8 servings

Presentation: Serve chilled with deli sandwiches or hamburgers.

Creamier Version: Prepare potatoes as above. Replace the vinegar and oil with
½ cup *each* mayonnaise, dairy sour cream and salsa. Mix with Taco Spices & Seasonings
and continue as directed above.

Potato-Bean Salad Vinaigrette ▶

1½ pounds unpeeled red-skinned
    potatoes, scrubbed and
    cubed
1½ teaspoons salt, divided
¼ cup olive oil
2 tablespoons red wine vinegar
1 clove garlic, minced
1 tablespoon minced fresh
    oregano *or* 1 teaspoon dried
    oregano leaves, crushed

¼ teaspoon black pepper
1 can (15 ounces) Great
    Northern beans, rinsed and
    drained
1 cup finely chopped celery
1 cup finely chopped red bell
    pepper
½ cup sliced ripe olives
    (optional)
¼ cup finely chopped red onion

1. Place potatoes in medium saucepan; add water to cover and 1 teaspoon salt. Bring to a boil over medium-high heat. Reduce heat to medium-low. Simmer; uncovered, 5 to 7 minutes until potatoes are tender when pierced with fork. (Do not overcook.) Drain.

2. Whisk together oil, vinegar, garlic, oregano, remaining ½ teaspoon salt and black pepper in large bowl until mixture thickens.

3. Add beans, celery, bell pepper, olives, if desired, and onion. Toss gently. Add warm potatoes; toss gently until vegetables are coated. Let salad stand at least 10 minutes to marinate. Serve warm or at room temperature.   *Makes 4 to 6 servings*

Tomato Potato Salad

1½ pounds fresh California
    tomatoes, seeded and cubed
½ cup chopped red onion
¼ cup chopped fresh cilantro
1½ teaspoons ground cumin

1 teaspoon chopped fresh garlic
¼ teaspoon black pepper
1½ pounds red potatoes, cooked
    and cubed
½ cup plain nonfat yogurt

Combine tomatoes, onion and seasonings in large bowl. Add potatoes and yogurt; gently toss to coat.   *Makes 6 to 8 servings*

Favorite recipe from ***California Tomato Board***

Grilled Steak & Potato Salad ▼

Marinade
- ¼ cup warm water
- 3 tablespoons herb-flavored oil*
- 2 tablespoons balsamic vinegar
- 2 tablespoons seasoned rice vinegar
- 1 teaspoon grainy Dijon mustard
- ¼ teaspoon salt

Salad
- 1 pound lean boneless top sirloin steak
- 4 medium Colorado Sangre red potatoes, scrubbed
- 2 small ears corn, quartered *or* 1 large ear, cut into eighths
- 1 small red bell pepper, cut into rings or strips
- 1 large zucchini, sliced
- 8 medium mushrooms, halved
- ½ red onion, sliced
- Salt and black pepper
- Salad greens

To prepare marinade, whisk together marinade ingredients in bowl. Place steak in large resealable plastic food storage bag. Add about 2 tablespoons marinade. Seal bag. Marinate in refrigerator 1 hour or longer.

Meanwhile, steam or microwave potatoes until tender; cool. Cut potatoes into thick slices or chunks; arrange potatoes, corn, bell pepper, zucchini, mushrooms and onion in rows in glass 13×9-inch baking dish. Add remaining marinade. Marinate 30 minutes or longer. Remove vegetables from marinade, reserving marinade. Grill vegetables over hot coals until tender. Season to taste with salt. Remove steak from marinade, discarding any remaining marinade. Season to taste with salt and pepper. Grill over hot coals to desired doneness. Place salad greens on each of four serving plates. Arrange vegetables on greens. Slice steak on the diagonal and arrange on plates. Pour reserved marinade over salad.   *Makes 4 servings*

*Olive oil combined with your choice of chopped fresh herbs or dried herb leaves can be substituted for herb-flavored oil.

Nutrients per serving: *Calories: 452, Total Fat: 16 g, Cholesterol: 77 mg, Sodium: 345 mg, Protein: 33 g, Dietary Fiber: 6 g*

Favorite recipe from **Colorado Potato Administrative Committee**

Gloria's Pesto Potato Salad

Dressing

   1 cup mayonnaise

   2 tablespoons prepared pesto

Salad

   4 cups diced peeled cooked
      potatoes

   ½ cup chopped celery

½ cup sliced green onions

½ cup diced red bell pepper

1½ cups (6 ounces) cubed
   Wisconsin Monterey Jack
   cheese

1 tablespoon grated Wisconsin
   Parmesan cheese

Combine dressing ingredients in small bowl. Combine potatoes, celery, onions, pepper and Monterey Jack cheese in medium bowl. Add dressing; toss lightly. Sprinkle with Parmesan cheese. Chill.   *Makes 6 servings*

Tip: Wisconsin Havarti cheese delivers the same creamy texture as Monterey Jack cheese and can be substituted for it in this recipe.

Favorite recipe from **Wisconsin Milk Marketing Board**

Potato Salad with Sweet Sausages and Mushrooms

3 pounds (16 to 20) small red potatoes, scrubbed and quartered

2 pounds sweet Italian sausages

½ cup dry red wine

⅔ cup plus 2 tablespoons extra-virgin olive oil, divided

1 pound mushrooms, sliced

1 teaspoon lemon juice

3 teaspoons TABASCO® pepper sauce, divided

¾ cup chopped green onions

⅓ cup dry white wine

⅓ cup chicken broth or stock

2 tablespoons Dijon mustard

½ teaspoon salt

¼ teaspoon black pepper

Cook potatoes in boiling water in large saucepan 15 to 20 minutes or until fork tender. Drain and cool. Cut into ¼-inch-thick slices. Place in large bowl.

Meanwhile, preheat oven to 350°F. Place sausages in single layer in baking dish; pierce several times with fork. Bake 15 minutes. Turn and bake 15 minutes longer. Add red wine; turn sausages. Bake 8 minutes. Turn sausages once more; bake 7 minutes longer or until cooked through. Remove sausages; cool. Cut into 1-inch-thick slices. Add to potatoes.

Heat 2 tablespoons olive oil in large skillet over medium-high heat. Add mushrooms; cook and stir 5 minutes or until most of liquid evaporates. Sprinkle with lemon juice and 1½ teaspoon TABASCO sauce. Add to potato mixture with green onions; toss lightly to mix.

Combine white wine, broth, mustard, salt, pepper and remaining 1½ teaspoons TABASCO sauce in food processor or blender. Process until well blended. While food processor is running, slowly add remaining ⅔ cup olive oil; process until blended. Pour mixture over salad; toss to coat. Serve warm or at room temperature; or cover and refrigerate overnight. *Makes 12 servings*

SPAM™ Skillet Potato Salad

1 (12-ounce) can SPAM®
　　Luncheon Meat, cut into
　　strips
½ cup chopped green onions
½ cup chopped green bell pepper
3 medium potatoes, boiled and
　　diced

1½ cups (6 ounces) shredded
　　sharp Cheddar cheese
¼ cup mayonnaise or salad
　　dressing

In large skillet over medium heat, sauté SPAM,® green onions and bell pepper until
SPAM® is lightly browned. Add potatoes, cheese and mayonnaise. Heat just until cheese
begins to melt.　　　　　　　　　　　　　　　　　　　　　　*Makes 6 servings*

*Nutrients per serving: Calories: 353, Total Fat: 25 g, Cholesterol: 80 mg, Sodium: 792 mg,
Protein: 18 g*

Wisconsin True Blue Potato Salad

1¼ cups dairy sour cream
2 tablespoons minced parsley
2 tablespoons tarragon-flavored
　　white wine vinegar
½ teaspoon salt
½ teaspoon celery seed
⅛ teaspoon black pepper

¾ cup (3-ounces) crumbled
　　Wisconsin Blue cheese
4 cups cubed cooked potatoes
½ cup sliced water chestnuts
½ cup diced celery
½ cup green onion slices

Combine sour cream, parsley, vinegar and seasonings in medium bowl; mix well. Stir in
cheese. Combine potatoes, water chestnuts, celery and onions in large bowl. Add sour
cream mixture; toss lightly. Chill.　　　　　　　　　　　　　　*Makes 6 servings*

*Nutrients per serving: Calories: 240, Total Fat: 14 g, Cholesterol: 32 mg, Sodium: 416 mg,
Protein: 6 g*

*Favorite recipe from **Wisconsin Milk Marketing Board***

Gourmet Deli Potato & Pea Salad ▶

1½ pounds new potatoes,
    scrubbed and quartered
1 cup water
¾ teaspoon salt, divided
½ pound sugar snap peas or
    snow peas, trimmed
⅓ cup reduced-fat mayonnaise

⅓ cup plain nonfat yogurt
3 tablespoons FRENCH'S® Dijon
    Mustard
⅓ cup finely chopped red onion
2 tablespoons minced dill *or*
    2 teaspoons dried dill weed
1 clove garlic, minced

Place potatoes, water and ½ *teaspoon* salt in 3-quart microwave-safe baking dish. Cover and microwave on HIGH 15 minutes or until potatoes are tender, stirring once. Add peas. Cover and microwave on HIGH 3 minutes or until peas are crisp-tender. Rinse with cold water and drain. Cool completely.

Combine mayonnaise, yogurt and mustard in large bowl until blended. Stir in onion, dill, garlic and remaining ¼ *teaspoon* salt. Add potatoes and peas; toss to coat evenly. Cover and refrigerate 1 hour before serving. *Makes 6 side-dish servings*

Prep Time: 15 minutes   **Cook Time:** 18 minutes   **Chill Time:** 1 hour

German Potato Salad

4 cups sliced, peeled Colorado
    potatoes
4 slices bacon
¾ cup chopped onion
¼ cup sugar
3 tablespoons all-purpose flour

1½ teaspoons salt
1 teaspoon celery seeds
¼ teaspoon black pepper
1 cup water
¾ cup vinegar
2 hard-cooked eggs, chopped

Cook potatoes in boiling water until tender; drain. Meanwhile, cook bacon in medium skillet. Drain on paper towels; cool and crumble. Cook and stir onion in drippings until tender. Combine sugar, flour, salt, celery seeds and pepper, blend in water and vinegar. Stir into onion in skillet; heat until bubbly. Pour over combined potatoes, bacon and eggs; toss. Serve immediately. *Makes 6 servings*

Nutrients per serving: Calories: 282, Total Fat: 14 g, Cholesterol: 84 mg, Sodium: 679 mg, Protein: 6 g, Dietary Fiber: 2 g

*Favorite recipe from **Colorado Potato Administrative Committee***

POTATOES
Take Center Stage

Potatoes have a natural affinity for meat, poultry and cheese. Stuff them with spicy meat or poultry mixtures or combine them with zesty baked chicken, cheesy pork chops or herb-crusted roast beef for main dishes that will steal the show.

Baked Potatoes with Tuna and Broccoli in Cheese Sauce ▶

2 medium baking potatoes (6 to 8 ounces each)
1 package (10 ounces) frozen broccoli in cheese sauce
1 can (6 ounces) STARKIST® Solid White Tuna, drained and chunked

1 teaspoon chili powder
¼ cup minced green onions, including tops
2 slices cooked, crumbled bacon

Microwave Directions: Wash and pierce potatoes; microwave on HIGH 8 minutes. Remove from microwave. Wrap in foil; let stand to finish cooking while preparing broccoli. Microwave vented pouch of broccoli on HIGH 5 minutes. In medium microwavable bowl, combine tuna and chili powder. Gently stir in broccoli. Cover; heat on HIGH 1½ more minutes or until heated through. Cut potatoes in half lengthwise. Top with broccoli-tuna mixture; sprinkle with onions and bacon.   *Makes 2 servings*

Prep Time: 20 minutes

Note: Recipe can easily be doubled for 4—just cook a little longer in the microwave.

Potato Straw Cake with Ham & Gruyère ▶

4 medium Colorado russet
   variety potatoes
1 tablespoon water
2 teaspoons lemon juice
2 teaspoons Dijon mustard
1 cup (4 ounces) thinly sliced
   ham, cut into strips
¾ cup (3 ounces) shredded
   Gruyère cheese

½ teaspoon dried tarragon,
   crushed *or* ¼ teaspoon
   ground nutmeg
3 to 4 green onions, thinly
   sliced, white parts separated
   from dark green tops
3 teaspoons oil, divided
   Salt and black pepper

Peel and grate potatoes. Place in bowl with water to cover; let stand at room temperature about ½ hour while preparing other ingredients. Blend 1 tablespoon water, lemon juice and mustard in bowl. Stir in ham, cheese, tarragon and white parts of onions. Reserve green onion tops. Drain potatoes, wrap in several thicknesses of paper towels or clean dish towel and squeeze to wring out much of liquid.

Heat 1½ teaspoons oil in heavy 8- or 10-inch nonstick skillet over high heat. Add half the potatoes, pressing into skillet with back of spoon. Season to taste with salt and pepper. Spread evenly with ham mixture. Cover with remaining potatoes. Season to taste with salt and pepper. Reduce heat to medium-low. Cover and cook 20 to 30 minutes or until potatoes are crisp and golden brown on bottom. Uncover and place rimless baking sheet over skillet. Invert skillet onto baking sheet to release potato cake. Add remaining 1½ teaspoons oil to skillet. Slide cake into skillet, uncooked side down. Cook, uncovered, over medium-low heat 10 to 15 minutes. Increase heat to medium-high and cook until brown and crisp, shaking pan several times to prevent sticking. Slide potato cake onto serving plate. Garnish with reserved green onion tops. Cut into wedges.

Makes 5 to 6 servings

Nutrients per serving *(¹/₅ of recipe): Calories: 204, Total Fat: 8 g, Cholesterol: 26 mg, Sodium: 305 mg, Protein: 11 g, Dietary Fiber: 2 g*

Favorite recipe from **Colorado Potato Administrative Committee**

Tex-Mex Ground Turkey Potato Boats ▲

2 medium potatoes
½ pound ground turkey
½ cup onion, chopped
1 clove garlic, minced
1 can (8 ounces) stewed
    tomatoes
1 teaspoon chili powder

¼ teaspoon salt
¼ teaspoon dried oregano leaves,
    crushed
¼ teaspoon ground cumin
¼ teaspoon red pepper flakes
½ cup (2 ounces) shredded
    reduced-fat Cheddar cheese

1. Preheat oven to 400°F. Pierce potatoes several times with fork. Bake 50 to 60 minutes or until soft. Cool slightly. *Reduce oven temperature to 375°F.*

2. Slice potatoes in half, lengthwise. Scoop out pulp with spoon, leaving ¼-inch shell. (Reserve potato pulp for other use.) Place potato shells on jelly-roll pan or baking sheet.

3. Place turkey, onion and garlic in medium skillet. Cook over medium-high heat 5 minutes or until turkey is no longer pink; drain. Add tomatoes, chili powder, salt, oregano, cumin and red pepper flakes to turkey in skillet. Cook 15 minutes or until most of liquid has evaporated.

4. Spoon turkey mixture evenly into potato shells; sprinkle with cheese. Bake 15 minutes or until cheese melts. *Makes 4 servings*

Nutrients per serving: Calories: 209, Total Fat: 7 g, Cholesterol: 51 mg, Sodium: 446 mg, Protein: 16 g

Favorite recipe from **National Turkey Federation**

Herb-Crusted Roast Beef and Potatoes

1 (4½-pound) eye of round or sirloin tip beef roast
¾ cup plus 2 tablespoons FILIPPO BERIO® Olive Oil, divided
Salt and freshly ground black pepper
2 tablespoons paprika

2 pounds small red-skin potatoes, cut in half
1 cup dry bread crumbs
1 teaspoon dried thyme leaves
1 teaspoon dried rosemary
½ teaspoon salt
¼ teaspoon freshly ground black pepper

Preheat oven to 325°F. Brush roast with 2 tablespoons olive oil. Season to taste with salt and pepper. Place in large roasting pan; insert meat thermometer into center of thickest part of roast. Roast 45 minutes.

Meanwhile, in large bowl, combine ½ cup olive oil and paprika. Add potatoes; toss until lightly coated. In small bowl, combine bread crumbs, thyme, rosemary, ½ teaspoon salt, ¼ teaspoon pepper and remaining ¼ cup olive oil.

Carefully remove roast from oven. Place potatoes around roast. Press bread crumb mixture onto top of roast to form crust. Sprinkle any remaining bread crumb mixture over potatoes. Roast an additional 40 to 45 minutes or until meat thermometer registers 145°F for medium-rare or until desired doneness is reached. Transfer roast to carving board; tent with foil. Let stand 5 to 10 minutes before carving. Cut into ¼-inch-thick slices. Serve immediately with potatoes, spooning any bread crumb mixture from roasting pan onto meat. *Makes 8 servings*

Scallop Supper

1 pound cooked bay or calico
   scallops
6 medium baking potatoes,
   scrubbed
¼ cup margarine or butter,
   melted

¼ cup all-purpose flour
1 teaspoon salt
2 cups milk
1 cup cooked frozen green peas
   Paprika for garnish

Preheat oven to 425°F. Pierce potatoes several times with fork. Bake 45 to 60 minutes or until soft.

Melt margarine in saucepan over low heat. Blend in flour and salt; cook 2 minutes. Gradually add milk; cook over medium heat until thick and smooth, stirring constantly. Stir in peas and scallops; cook just until peas are heated through. Make slit in top of each potato and squeeze ends to open. Top with scallop mixture. Sprinkle with paprika.

Makes 6 servings

Favorite recipe from **Florida Department of Agriculture and Consumer Services, Bureau of Seafood and Aquaculture**

Sweet Potato Turkey Pie ▶

1 can (24 ounces) sweet
   potatoes, drained
2 tablespoons margarine, melted
¼ teaspoon pumpkin pie spice
2 cups cooked turkey, cut into
   ½- to ¾-inch cubes
1 can (10¾ ounces) reduced-fat,
   reduced-sodium cream-style
   mushroom soup
1 package (9 ounces) frozen
   French-style green beans,
   thawed and drained

1 can (2 ounces) mushroom
   stems and pieces, drained
½ teaspoon salt
½ teaspoon black pepper
2 tablespoons canned fried
   onion rings, crushed
1 can (8 ounces) whole
   cranberry sauce (optional)

1. Preheat oven to 350°F. Lightly spray 9-inch pie plate with nonstick cooking spray.

2. Beat sweet potatoes, margarine and pumpkin pie spice in medium bowl with electric mixer at low speed until smooth. Spread potato mixture in prepared pan to form crust.

3. Combine turkey, soup, beans, mushrooms, salt and pepper in medium bowl until blended. Pour mixture into prepared crust. Sprinkle with onions. Bake 30 minutes or until hot. Serve with cranberry sauce, if desired. *Makes 6 servings*

Nutrients per serving: *Calories: 262, Total Fat: 8 g, Cholesterol: 36 mg, Sodium: 553 mg, Protein: 17 g*

*Favorite recipe from **National Turkey Federation***

Potatoes Take Center Stage **51**

Country Kielbasa Kabobs ▶

½ cup GREY POUPON® COUNTRY
   DIJON® Mustard
½ cup apricot preserves
⅓ cup minced green onions
1 pound kielbasa, cut into 1-inch
   pieces
1 large apple, cored and cut into
   wedges

½ cup frozen pearl onions,
   thawed
6 small red skin potatoes,
   parboiled and cut into
   halves
3 cups shredded red and green
   cabbage, steamed

Soak 6 (10-inch) wooden skewers in water for 30 minutes. In small bowl, blend mustard, preserves and green onions; set aside ¼ cup mixture.

Alternately thread kielbasa, apple, pearl onions and potatoes on skewers. Grill or broil kabobs for 12 to 15 minutes or until done, turning and brushing with remaining mustard mixture. Heat reserved mustard mixture and toss with steamed cabbage. Serve heated through with kabobs. Garnish as desired. *Makes 6 servings*

Easy Chicken and Potato Dinner

1 package (2 pounds) bone-in
   chicken breasts or thighs
1 pound potatoes, cut into
   wedges
½ cup KRAFT® Zesty Italian
   Dressing

1 tablespoon Italian seasoning
½ cup KRAFT® 100% Grated
   Parmesan Cheese

PLACE chicken and potatoes in 13×9-inch baking pan.

POUR dressing over chicken and potatoes. Sprinkle evenly with Italian seasoning and cheese.

BAKE at 400°F for 1 hour or until chicken is cooked through. *Makes 4 servings*

Pork with Couscous & Root Vegetables ▶

1 teaspoon vegetable oil
½ pound pork tenderloin, thinly sliced
2 sweet potatoes, peeled and cut into chunks
2 medium turnips, peeled and cut into chunks
1 carrot, sliced
3 cloves garlic, finely chopped
1 can (about 15 ounces) chick-peas rinsed and drained
1 cup reduced-sodium vegetable broth
½ cup pitted prunes, cut into thirds
1 teaspoon ground cumin
½ teaspoon ground cinnamon
¼ teaspoon ground allspice
¼ teaspoon ground nutmeg
¼ teaspoon black pepper
1 cup cooked couscous
2 tablespoons dried currants

1. Heat oil in large nonstick skillet over medium-high heat until hot. Add pork, sweet potatoes, turnips, carrot and garlic. Cook and stir 5 minutes. Stir in chick-peas, broth, prunes, cumin, cinnamon, allspice, nutmeg and pepper. Cover; bring to a boil over high heat. Reduce heat to medium-low. Simmer 30 minutes until vegetables are tender.

2. Serve pork and vegetables on couscous. Top servings evenly with currants. Garnish with fresh thyme, if desired.   *Makes 4 servings*

Nutrients per serving: *Calories: 508, Total Fat: 6 g, Saturated Fat: 1 g, Cholesterol: 30 mg, Sodium: 500 mg, Protein: 26 g, Dietary Fiber: 17 g*

Potato & Lamb Cobbler

1¼ pounds boneless American lamb (leg or shoulder), cut into ¾-inch pieces
¼ cup all-purpose flour
2 teaspoons olive oil
2 cups lamb stock *or* 1 can (14½ ounces) beef broth plus ¼ cup water, divided
¾ pound mushrooms (wild or cultivated), sliced
1 onion, chopped
2 garlic cloves, minced
1 pound red-skinned potatoes, cut into ¾-inch cubes

1½ teaspoons chopped fresh thyme *or* 1 teaspoon dried thyme leaves, crushed
1½ teaspoons chopped fresh rosemary *or* 1 teaspoon dried rosemary, crushed
3 tablespoons finely chopped fresh parsley
Cobbler Dough (recipe follows)
1 egg yolk
1 tablespoon milk

Season lamb to taste with salt and pepper; coat with flour. Heat oil in Dutch oven over medium-high heat. Add lamb and brown on all sides. Remove lamb from pan and reserve. Add ½ cup stock, mushrooms, onion and garlic; cook until liquid has evaporated and onion is tender, stirring to scrape all brown bits from pan. Add remaining 1½ cups stock, potatoes, thyme and rosemary; cover and bring to a boil. Reduce heat to low; add lamb. Simmer, partially covered, 45 minutes or until lamb is tender. Season to taste with additional salt and pepper, if desired. Stir in chopped parsley.*

Preheat oven to 375°F. Prepare Cobbler Dough. On a lightly floured surface, roll dough to about ¼-inch thickness. Using a cookie cutter, cut dough into leaves or other shapes; reroll scraps and cut more shapes. Ladle lamb mixture into 1½-quart casserole or 10-inch deep-dish pie plate. Top with dough cutouts, clustering and overlapping leaves slightly, allowing open spaces for steam to escape. Beat together egg yolk and milk; brush dough with mixture. Bake about 15 to 20 minutes or until top is golden brown.

Makes 6 servings

*Sauce should be the consistency of gravy. If it's too thin, remove lamb and vegetables to casserole with a slotted spoon. Boil the sauce to reduce it to desired consistency.

Cobbler Dough: Combine 1 cup flour, 1 tablespoon sugar, 1 teaspoon baking powder and ½ teaspoon salt in a small bowl. Stir in ½ cup heavy cream; mix just until blended. Gather dough into ball.

*Favorite recipe from **American Lamb Council***

Cheesy Pork Chops 'n' Potatoes

1 jar (8 ounces) pasteurized processed cheese spread
1 tablespoon vegetable oil
6 thin pork chops, ¼ to ½ inch thick
Seasoned salt
½ cup milk

4 cups frozen cottage fries
1⅓ cups (2.8 ounce can) FRENCH'S® French Fried Onions
1 package (10 ounces) frozen broccoli spears,* thawed and drained

Preheat oven to 350°F. Spoon cheese spread into 8×12-inch baking dish; place in oven just until cheese melts, about 5 minutes. Meanwhile, in large skillet, heat oil. Brown pork chops on both sides; drain. Sprinkle chops with seasoned salt; set aside. Using fork, stir milk into melted cheese until well blended. Stir cottage fries and ⅔ *cup* French Fried Onions into cheese mixture. Divide broccoli spears into 6 small bunches. Arrange bunches of spears over potato mixture with flowerets around edges of dish. Arrange chops over broccoli *stalks*. Bake, covered, at 350°F for 35 to 40 minutes or until pork chops are no longer pink. Top chops with remaining ⅔ *cup* onions; bake, uncovered, 5 minutes or until onions are golden brown. *Makes 4 to 6 servings*

*1 small head fresh broccoli (about ½ pound) may be substituted for frozen spears. Divide into spears and cook 3 to 4 minutes before using.

Microwave Directions: Omit oil. Reduce milk to ¼ cup. In 8×12-inch microwave-safe dish, place cheese spread and milk. Cook, covered, on HIGH 3 minutes; stir to blend. Stir in cottage fries and ⅔ *cup* onions. Cook, covered, 5 minutes; stir. Top with broccoli spears as above. Arrange unbrowned pork chops over broccoli *stalks* with meatiest parts toward edges of dish. Cook, covered, on MEDIUM (50-60%) 24 to 30 minutes or until pork chops are no longer pink. Turn chops over, sprinkle with seasoned salt and rotate dish halfway through cooking time. Top with remaining ⅔ *cup* onions; cook, uncovered, on HIGH 1 minute. Let stand 5 minutes.

Sweet Potato Soufflé ▶

5 tablespoons butter or
    margarine, divided
1½ pounds sweet potatoes, peeled
    and cut into 1-inch cubes
⅓ cup firmly packed brown sugar
¼ cup dry sherry
1 teaspoon ground cinnamon

½ teaspoon ground nutmeg
1 cup milk
3 tablespoons all-purpose flour
½ teaspoon salt
3 egg yolks
5 egg whites

1. Preheat oven to 400°F. Grease 2-quart soufflé dish with 1 tablespoon butter.

2. Place potatoes in 3-quart saucepan; add water to cover. Bring to a boil over high heat. Reduce heat to medium-low. Simmer, uncovered, 12 to 14 minutes until potatoes are fork-tender. Drain. Transfer potatoes to large bowl; mash with potato masher until smooth. Stir in sugar, sherry, cinnamon and nutmeg until well blended; set aside.

3. Heat milk in small saucepan over medium heat until warm. Melt remaining 4 tablespoons butter in 2-quart saucepan over medium heat. Reduce heat to low; stir in flour. Cook and stir 2 minutes or until completely smooth. Gradually whisk in warm milk until well blended. Add salt; whisk constantly over medium heat 2 to 3 minutes until sauce boils and thickens.

4. Whisk in egg yolks, 1 at a time, blending completely after each. Cook and stir 1 minute more. Add to potato mixture; mix well. Cool completely.

5. Meanwhile, beat egg whites in large bowl with electric mixer at high speed until stiff peaks form. Stir ⅓ beaten egg whites into cooled potato mixture with rubber spatula; fold in remaining egg whites.

6. Pour potato mixture into prepared dish, gently smoothing top with spatula. Place dish in center of oven; bake 10 minutes. *Reduce oven temperature to 375°F.* Bake 45 to 50 minutes longer until soufflé edge is puffy, center is set and top is lightly browned. Serve immediately.
Makes 6 servings

Mini Meat Loaves & Vegetables ▼

1½ pounds lean ground beef
1 egg
1 can (8 ounces) tomato sauce, divided
1⅓ cups (2.8 ounce can) FRENCH'S® French Fried Onions
½ teaspoon salt
½ teaspoon Italian seasoning

6 small red potatoes, thinly sliced (about 1½ cups)
1 bag (16 ounces) frozen vegetable combination (broccoli, corn, red pepper), thawed and drained
Salt
Black pepper

Preheat oven to 375°F. In medium bowl, combine ground beef, egg, ½ *can* tomato sauce, ⅔ *cup* French Fried Onions, ½ teaspoon salt and Italian seasoning. Shape into 3 mini loaves and place in 9×13-inch baking dish. Arrange potatoes around loaves. Bake, covered, at 375°F for 35 minutes. Spoon vegetables around meat loaves; stir to combine with potatoes. Lightly season vegetables with salt and pepper, if desired. Top meat loaves with remaining tomato sauce. Bake, uncovered, 15 minutes or until meat loaves are done. Top loaves with remaining ⅔ *cup* onions; bake, uncovered, 3 minutes or until onions are golden brown. *Makes 6 servings*

Microwave Directions: Prepare meat loaves as above. Arrange potatoes on bottom of 8×12-inch microwave-safe dish; place meat loaves on potatoes. Cook, covered, on HIGH 13 minutes. Rotate dish halfway through cooking time. Add vegetables and season as above. Top meat loaves with remaining tomato sauce. Cook, covered, 7 minutes or until meat loaves are done. Rotate dish halfway through cooking time. Top loaves with remaining ⅔ *cup* onions; cook, uncovered, 1 minute. Let stand 5 minutes.

Steak & Potato Stir-Fry

12 ounces boneless beef top
    round steak
½ cup water
3 tablespoons soy sauce
1 tablespoon cornstarch
¼ teaspoon black pepper
1 to 2 tablespoons vegetable or
    olive oil, divided
1 onion, cut into thin wedges

2 cloves garlic, minced
2 medium Colorado potatoes, cut
    into matchstick-size strips
1 green bell pepper, cut into
    1-inch squares
2 medium tomatoes, cut into thin
    wedges
Chow mein noodles (optional)

Trim fat from meat. Thinly slice across the grain into bite-size strips. For sauce, in small bowl stir together water, soy sauce, cornstarch and black pepper. Set aside. In large skillet or wok, heat 1 tablespoon oil. Add onion and garlic; stir-fry over medium-high heat 5 minutes or until almost tender. Add potatoes; stir-fry over medium heat 5 minutes or until almost tender. Add bell pepper; stir-fry 2 minutes longer or until vegetables are tender. Remove vegetable mixture from skillet. Heat remaining 1 tablespoon oil in skillet over medium-high heat, if necessary. Add beef; stir-fry 2 minutes. Return vegetable mixture to skillet. Push mixture from center of skillet. Stir sauce; add to center of skillet. Cook and stir until thickened. Stir in tomatoes until beef and vegetables are coated. Cook just until tomatoes are heated through. Serve immediately over chow mein noodles, if desired. *Makes 4 servings*

Nutrients per serving: Calories: 249, Total Fat: 7 g, Cholesterol: 53 mg, Sodium: 821 mg, Protein: 23 g, Dietary Fiber: 3 g

*Favorite recipe from **Colorado Potato Administrative Committee***

Oven-Easy Beef

4 cups frozen hash brown
   potatoes, thawed
3 tablespoons vegetable oil
⅛ teaspoon black pepper
1 pound ground beef
1 cup water
1 package (about ¾ ounce)
   brown gravy mix
½ teaspoon garlic salt

1 package (10 ounces) frozen
   mixed vegetables, thawed
   and drained
1 cup (4 ounces) shredded
   Cheddar cheese
1⅓ cups (2.8 ounce can)
   FRENCH'S® French Fried
   Onions

Preheat oven to 400°F. In 8×12-inch baking dish, combine potatoes, oil and pepper. Firmly press potato mixture evenly across bottom and up sides of dish to form a shell. Bake, uncovered, at 400°F for 15 minutes. Meanwhile, in large skillet, brown ground beef; drain. Stir in water, gravy mix and garlic salt; bring to a boil. Add mixed vegetables; reduce heat to medium and cook, uncovered, 5 minutes. Remove from heat and stir in *½ cup* cheese and *⅔ cup* French Fried Onions; spoon into hot potato shell. *Reduce oven temperature to 350°F.* Bake, uncovered, at 350°F for 15 minutes or until heated through. Top with remaining cheese and *⅔ cup* onions; bake, uncovered, 5 minutes or until onions are golden brown.   *Makes 4 to 6 servings*

Pizza-Style Stuffed Potatoes ▶

½ pound lean ground American
   lamb
4 large baking potatoes,
   scrubbed
⅓ cup finely chopped onion
⅓ cup chopped green bell pepper
¼ cup chopped mushrooms
2 teaspoons dried parsley flakes
2 teaspoons Italian seasoning
½ teaspoon garlic powder

½ cup plain nonfat yogurt
½ teaspoon salt
¼ teaspoon black pepper
1 cup (4 ounces) shredded
   reduced-fat mozzarella
   cheese, divided
½ cup pizza sauce
12 sliced black olives (optional)
2 tablespoons grated Parmesan
   cheese

Pierce potatoes several times with fork. Microwave on paper towel at HIGH 10 to 12 minutes or until potatoes are soft. Cool slightly.

Preheat oven to 400°F. Cook lamb in medium skillet over medium heat until no longer pink; drain. Add onion, bell pepper and mushrooms; microwave at HIGH 2 minutes. Stir in parsley, Italian seasoning and garlic powder.

Make lengthwise slit in each potato. Scoop out pulp leaving shells intact. Place pulp in medium bowl. Beat in yogurt, salt and black pepper. Add ⅔ cup mozzarella cheese and ground lamb mixture; mix until blended. Spoon mixture into potato shells. Top each potato with pizza sauce, remaining ⅓ cup mozzarella cheese, olives, if desired, and Parmesan cheese.* Bake 20 minutes or until hot and bubbly. *Makes 4 servings*

*Stuffed potatoes can be wrapped in foil and frozen before baking. To serve, thaw in refrigerator and bake as directed.

Nutrition per serving: *Calories: 408, Total Fat: 16 g, Cholesterol: 56 mg, Sodium: 782 mg*

Favorite recipe from **American Lamb Council**

POTATOES
in Supporting Roles

Potato side dishes are perfect co-stars for your favorite entrées. Try these satisfying casseroles, great gratins and fresh-from-the-grill accompaniments.

Fresh Vegetable Casserole ▶

8 small new potatoes, scrubbed
8 baby carrots
1 small cauliflower, broken into
   florets
4 stalks asparagus, cut into
   1-inch pieces
3 tablespoons margarine or
   butter

3 tablespoons all-purpose flour
2 cups milk
   Salt
   Black pepper
¾ cup (3 ounces) shredded
   Cheddar cheese
   Chopped fresh cilantro

Preheat oven to 350°F. Cook vegetables until crisp-tender. Arrange vegetables in greased 2-quart casserole. To make sauce, melt margarine in medium saucepan over medium heat. Stir in flour until smooth; cook 2 minutes. Gradually stir in milk. Cook until thickened, stirring constantly. Season to taste with salt and pepper. Add cheese, stirring until cheese is melted. Pour sauce over vegetables and sprinkle with cilantro. Bake 15 minutes or until heated through. *Makes 4 to 6 servings*

Potato Latkes ▶

⅔ cup EGG BEATERS® Healthy
  Real Egg Product
⅓ cup all-purpose flour
¼ cup grated onion
¼ teaspoon ground black pepper
4 large potatoes, peeled and
  shredded (about 4 cups)

3 tablespoons FLEISCHMANN'S®
  Margarine, divided
1½ cups sweetened applesauce
Fresh chives, for garnish

In large bowl, combine Egg Beaters, flour, onion and pepper; set aside.

Pat shredded potatoes dry with paper towels. Stir into egg mixture. In large nonstick skillet, over medium-high heat, melt 1½ tablespoons margarine. For each pancake, spoon about ⅓ cup potato mixture into skillet, spreading into 4-inch circle. Cook for 3 minutes on each side or until golden; remove and keep warm. Repeat with remaining mixture, using remaining margarine as needed to make 12 pancakes. Serve hot with applesauce. Garnish with chives. *Makes 4 servings*

Prep Time: 20 minutes   **Cook Time:** 18 minutes

Nutrients per serving: Calories: 460, Total Fat: 12 g, Saturated Fat: 4 g, Cholesterol: 0 mg, Sodium: 208 mg, Dietary Fiber: 4 g

Sweet Potato-Cranberry Bake

1 can (40 ounces) whole sweet
  potatoes, drained
1⅓ cups (2.8 ounce can)
  FRENCH'S® French Fried
  Onions

2 cups fresh cranberries
2 tablespoons packed brown
  sugar
⅓ cup honey

Preheat oven to 400°F. In 1½-quart casserole, layer sweet potatoes, *⅔ cup* French Fried Onions and *1 cup* cranberries. Sprinkle with brown sugar; drizzle with *half* the honey. Top with remaining cranberries and honey. Bake, covered, at 400° for 35 minutes or until heated through. Gently stir casserole. Top with remaining *⅔ cup* onions; bake, uncovered, 1 to 3 minutes or until onions are golden brown.

Makes 4 to 6 servings

Zippy Scalloped Potatoes ▼

Nonstick cooking spray
3 large baking potatoes (about 2½ pounds)
1 jar (11.5 ounces) GUILTLESS GOURMET® Nacho Dip (mild or spicy)

¾ cup skim milk
Fresh cilantro leaves and red pepper strips (optional)

MICROWAVE DIRECTIONS: Preheat oven to 350°F. Coat microwave-safe 2-quart rectangular dish or round casserole with cooking spray. Scrub potatoes with vegetable brush; thinly slice potatoes. (Slice in food processor, if desired.) Layer in prepared dish. Cover with vented plastic wrap or lid; microwave on HIGH (100% power) 10 minutes or until potatoes are fork-tender.

Combine nacho dip and milk in 4-cup glass measure; microwave on HIGH 2 minutes. Pour over potatoes; gently stir to coat potato slices. Cover and bake 30 minutes. Uncover; bake 10 minutes more or until heated through. Let stand 5 minutes before serving. Garnish with cilantro and pepper, if desired. *Makes 8 servings*

Nutrients per serving: Calories: 184, Total Fat: trace, Saturated Fat: 0 g, Cholesterol: 0 mg, Sodium: 240 mg, Protein: 5 g, Dietary Fiber: 3 g

As Good As Mashed Potatoes
(but Fat Free!)

4 medium IDAHO® Potatoes
(about 1½ pounds)
1¼ cups water
4 cloves garlic, minced
4 tablespoons parsley, chopped
3 dashes hot pepper sauce

1 teaspoon salt
¼ cup nonfat sour cream
2 teaspoons prepared
horseradish
2 teaspoons grainy mustard
1 teaspoon yellow mustard

Peel potatoes, if desired. Cut into 1-inch cubes; place in medium saucepan. Add water, garlic, parsley, pepper sauce and salt. Bring to a boil over medium-high heat. Reduce heat to low. Cover and cook about 20 minutes, stirring and breaking potatoes up with fork, adding hot water if potatoes are too dry. Continue stirring and mashing potatoes for about 5 minutes until water is absorbed and potatoes are soft and lumpy. Remove from heat, stir in the sour cream, horseradish and mustards.   *Makes 4 to 6 servings*

Nutrients per serving: Calories: 110, Total Fat: 0 g, Cholesterol: 0 mg, Sodium: 447 mg, Protein: 3 g

*Favorite recipe from **Idaho® Potato***

Herb Roasted Potatoes

½ cup MIRACLE WHIP® or
MIRACLE WHIP LIGHT®
Dressing
1 tablespoon *each* dried
rosemary, garlic powder and
onion powder

1 teaspoon seasoned salt
1 tablespoon water
2 pound small red potatoes,
quartered

MIX dressing, seasonings and water in large bowl. Add potatoes; toss to coat. Place potatoes on greased cookie sheet.

BAKE at 400°F for 30 to 40 minutes or until golden brown, stirring after 15 minutes.
Makes 8 servings

Note: Substitute dried oregano leaves for dried rosemary, if desired.

Prep Time: 15 minutes   **Baking Time:** 40 minutes

Savory Grilled Potatoes in Foil ▶

½ cup **MIRACLE WHIP®** Salad
   Dressing
3 garlic cloves, minced
½ teaspoon paprika

¼ teaspoon *each:* salt, pepper
3 baking potatoes, cut into
   ¼-inch slices
1 large onion, sliced

MIX salad dressing and seasonings in large bowl until well blended. Stir in potatoes and onions to coat.

DIVIDE potato mixture evenly among six 12-inch square pieces of heavy-duty foil. Seal each to form packet.

PLACE foil packets on grill over medium-hot coals (coals will have slight glow). Grill, covered, 25 to 30 minutes or until potatoes are tender.

Makes 6 side-dish servings

Prep Time: 15 minutes   **Grilling Time:** 30 minutes

Sautéed Garlic Potatoes

2 pounds boiling potatoes,
   peeled and cut into 1-inch
   pieces
3 tablespoons **FILIPPO BERIO®**
   Olive Oil
6 cloves garlic, skins on
1 tablespoon lemon juice

1 tablespoon chopped fresh
   chives
1 tablespoon chopped fresh
   parsley
Salt and freshly ground black
   pepper

Place potatoes in large colander; rinse under cold running water. Drain well; pat dry. In large nonstick skillet, heat olive oil over medium heat until hot. Add potatoes in a single layer. Cook, stirring and turning frequently, 10 minutes or until golden brown. Add garlic. Cover; reduce heat to low and cook very gently, shaking pan and stirring mixture occasionally, 15 to 20 minutes or until potatoes are tender when pierced with fork. Remove garlic; discard skins. In small bowl, crush garlic; stir in lemon juice. Add to potatoes; mix well. Cook 1 to 2 minutes or until heated through. Transfer to serving dish; sprinkle with chives and parsley. Season to taste with salt and pepper.

Makes 4 servings

Potato Gnocchi with Tomato Sauce ▶

2 pounds baking potatoes,
   scrubbed (3 or 4 large)
Tomato Sauce (recipe follows)
   or bottled meatless spaghetti
   sauce
²⁄₃ to 1 cup all-purpose flour,
   divided
1 egg yolk

½ teaspoon salt
⅛ teaspoon ground nutmeg
   (optional)
Freshly grated Parmesan
   cheese
Fresh basil leaves for garnish
   (optional)

1. Preheat oven to 425°F. Pierce potatoes several times with fork. Bake 1 hour or until soft. While potatoes are baking, prepare Tomato Sauce; set aside.

2. Cut baked potatoes in half lengthwise; cool slightly. Scoop pulp from skins with spoon into medium bowl; discard skins. Mash potatoes until smooth. Add ⅓ cup flour, egg yolk, salt and nutmeg, if desired, to potato pulp; mix well to form dough.

3. Turn out dough onto well floured surface. Knead in enough remaining flour to form smooth dough that is not sticky. Divide dough into 4 equal portions. Roll each portion with hands on lightly floured surface into long, ¾- to 1-inch-wide rope. Cut each rope into 1-inch pieces; gently press thumb into center of each piece to make indentation. Space gnocchi slightly apart on lightly floured kitchen towel to prevent them from sticking together.

4. Bring 4 quarts salted water to a gentle boil in Dutch oven over high heat. To test gnocchi cooking time, drop several gnocchi into water; cook 1 minute or until gnocchi float to surface. Remove from water with slotted spoon and taste for doneness. (If gnocchi start to dissolve, shorten cooking time by several seconds.) Cook remaining gnocchi in batches, removing with slotted spoon to warm serving dish.

5. Serve gnocchi immediately topped with warm Tomato Sauce and sprinkled with cheese. Garnish with basil, if desired.   *Makes 4 servings*

Tomato Sauce

- - - - - - - - - - - - - -

2 tablespoons olive oil or butter
1 clove garlic, minced
2 pounds ripe plum tomatoes,
    peeled, seeded and chopped
1 teaspoon sugar

¼ cup finely chopped prosciutto
    or cooked ham (optional)
1 tablespoon finely chopped
    fresh basil
Salt and black pepper to taste

1. Heat oil in medium saucepan over medium heat until hot. Add garlic; cook
30 seconds or until fragrant. Stir in tomatoes and sugar. Cook 10 minutes or until most
of liquid has evaporated. Stir in prosciutto, if desired, and basil. Cook 2 minutes. Season
to taste with salt and pepper.   *Makes about 2 cups*

Potato Gorgonzola Gratin

3 large Colorado russet potatoes,
   unpeeled and thinly sliced
Salt and black pepper
Ground nutmeg
½ medium onion, thinly sliced
1 medium tart green apple,* such
   as Granny Smith or Pippin,
   unpeeled, cored and thinly
   sliced

1 cup low-fat milk or half-and-
   half
3 ounces Gorgonzola or other
   blue cheese, crumbled
2 tablespoons grated Parmesan
   cheese

Preheat oven to 400°F. Arrange ½ of potatoes in 8- or 9-inch square baking dish. Season to taste with salt and pepper; sprinkle lightly with nutmeg. Top with onion and apple slices. Arrange remaining potatoes on top. Season to taste with additional salt and pepper. Pour milk over potato mixture. Cover dish with foil. Bake 30 to 40 minutes or until potatoes are tender. Remove foil; top with cheeses. Bake uncovered 10 to 15 minutes or until top is lightly brown in spots.   *Makes 4 to 6 servings*

*Substitute 1 medium pear for apple, if desired.

Nutrients per serving *(¼ of recipe): Calories: 153, Total Fat: 6 g, Cholesterol: 15 mg, Sodium: 254 mg, Protein: 7 g, Dietary Fiber: 2 g*

Favorite recipe from **Colorado Potato Administrative Committee**

Salsa Topped Baked Potatoes

4 large baking potatoes
2 tablespoons olive oil
1 large onion, diced
1 medium zucchini, diced
1 medium yellow squash, diced
2 large cloves garlic, minced
3 cups chopped ripe tomatoes
   (about 2 large)

¼ cup fresh basil
2 tablespoons red wine vinegar
1½ teaspoons TABASCO® pepper
   sauce
½ teaspoon salt

Preheat oven to 450°F. Pierce potatoes several times with fork. Place in shallow baking pan. Bake 45 minutes or until soft.

Meanwhile, to prepare salsa, heat oil in large skillet over medium heat. Add onion; cook and stir 5 minutes. Add zucchini, yellow squash and garlic; cook 3 minutes. Add tomatoes, basil, vinegar, TABASCO sauce and salt. Bring to a boil over high heat. Reduce heat to low. Simmer, uncovered, 5 minutes to blend flavors, stirring occasionally. Cut lengthwise slit in potatoes. Top with warm salsa. *Makes 4 servings*

Double-Baked Potatoes

3 large baking potatoes, scrubbed
¼ cup skim milk, warmed
1 cup (4 ounces) shredded reduced-fat Cheddar cheese
¾ cup whole kernel corn
1 tablespoon finely chopped fresh oregano *or* ½ teaspoon dried oregano leaves

½ teaspoon chili powder
Nonstick cooking spray
1 cup chopped onion
½ to 1 cup chopped poblano peppers
3 cloves garlic, minced
½ teaspoon salt
¼ teaspoon black pepper
3 tablespoons chopped fresh cilantro

1. Preheat oven to 400°F. Pierce potatoes several times with fork. Wrap each potato in foil. Bake about 1 hour or until soft. Cool slightly. *Reduce oven temperature to 350°F.*

2. Cut potatoes in half lengthwise; scoop out pulp with spoon leaving ¼-inch shells. Set shells aside. Beat potatoes in large bowl with electric mixer until coarsely mashed. Add milk; beat until smooth. Stir in cheese, corn, oregano and chili powder. Set aside.

3. Spray medium skillet with nonstick cooking spray. Add onion, poblano peppers and garlic; cook and stir 5 to 8 minutes or until tender. Stir in salt and black pepper.

4. Spoon potato mixture into potato shells. Sprinkle with onion mixture. Place stuffed potatoes in small baking pan. Bake 20 to 30 minutes or until heated through. Sprinkle with cilantro. *Makes 6 servings*

Nutrients per serving: Calories: 176, Total Fat: 3 g, Saturated Fat: 1 g, Cholesterol: 10 mg, Sodium: 451 mg, Protein: 7 g, Dietary Fiber: 1 g

Sweet Potato Gratin ▶

3 pounds sweet potatoes,
    scrubbed (about 4 to
    5 large)
½ cup margarine or butter,
    divided
¼ cup plus 2 tablespoons packed
    light brown sugar, divided
2 eggs
⅔ cup orange juice

2 teaspoons ground cinnamon,
    divided
½ teaspoon salt
¼ teaspoon ground nutmeg
⅓ cup all-purpose flour
¼ cup uncooked old-fashioned
    oats
⅓ cup chopped pecans or walnuts

1. Preheat oven to 350°F. Pierce potatoes several times with fork. Bake potatoes 1 hour or until soft. Or, microwave at HIGH 16 to 18 minutes, rotating and turning over after 9 minutes. Let stand 5 minutes.

2. Cut potatoes lengthwise into halves. Scrape pulp from skins into large bowl; discard skins. Beat ¼ cup margarine and 2 tablespoons sugar into potatoes with electric mixer at medium speed until margarine is melted. Beat in eggs, orange juice, 1½ teaspoons cinnamon, salt and nutmeg until smooth. Pour mixture into 1½-quart baking dish or gratin dish; smooth top.

3. For topping, combine flour, oats, remaining ¼ cup sugar and remaining ½ teaspoon cinnamon in medium bowl. Cut in remaining ¼ cup margarine with pastry blender or 2 knives until mixture becomes coarse crumbs. Stir in pecans. Sprinkle topping evenly over potato mixture.

4. Bake 25 to 30 minutes in 350°F oven or until heated through. For crisper topping, broil 5 inches from heat 2 to 3 minutes or until golden brown.

Makes 6 to 8 servings

Note: Gratin may be prepared a day ahead. Complete through step 3, cover and refrigerate.

Grilled Cajun Potato Wedges ▶

3 large baking potatoes,
　　scrubbed (about 2 pounds)
¼ cup olive oil
2 cloves garlic, minced
1 teaspoon salt
1 teaspoon paprika

½ teaspoon dried thyme leaves
½ teaspoon dried oregano leaves
¼ teaspoon black pepper
⅛ to ¼ teaspoon ground red
　　pepper

Prepare grill. Preheat oven to 425°F. Meanwhile, cut potatoes in half lengthwise, then cut each half lengthwise into 4 wedges. Place potatoes in large bowl. Add oil and garlic; toss to coat well. Combine salt, paprika, thyme, oregano, black pepper and red pepper in small bowl. Sprinkle over potatoes; toss to coat well. Place potato wedges in single layer in shallow roasting pan. (Reserve remaining oil mixture left in large bowl.) Bake 20 minutes. Meanwhile, cover 2 cups mesquite chips with cold water; soak 20 minutes.

Drain mesquite chips; sprinkle over coals. Place potato wedges on their sides on grid. Grill on covered grill over medium coals 15 to 20 minutes or until potatoes are brown and fork-tender, brushing with reserved oil mixture halfway through grilling time and turning once.

Makes 4 to 6 side-dish servings

New Potatoes with Crushed Red Peppers

1½ tablespoons BERTOLLI® Extra
　　Virgin or Classico Olive Oil
2 pounds small red new
　　potatoes, rinsed and
　　quartered

½ teaspoon crushed hot red
　　pepper
Salt and freshly ground black
　　pepper

1. Heat oil in nonstick skillet until hot enough to sizzle when piece of potato added. Add potatoes; turn the heat to medium-high and cook the potatoes, turning often, until evenly browned.

2. Sprinkle with the crushed red pepper; cover and cook until the potatoes are tender, about 10 minutes. Sprinkle with salt and pepper.

Makes 4 servings

Nutrients per serving: Calories: 229, Total Fat: 6 g, Saturated Fat: 1 g, Monounsaturated Fat: 4 g, Cholesterol: 0 mg, Sodium: 18 mg, Protein: 4 g, Dietary Fiber: 4 g

RISE & SHINE
Brunch Dishes

Potatoes have always been a popular accompaniment to breakfast eggs. Now discover how they can add excitement to brunch dishes, such as omelets, frittatas, quiches and quick breads.

Potato-Carrot Pancakes ▶

1 pound baking potatoes, peeled (3 medium)
1 medium carrot
2 tablespoons minced green onion

1 tablespoon all-purpose flour
1 egg, beaten
½ teaspoon salt
⅛ teaspoon black pepper
2 tablespoons vegetable oil

1. Shred potatoes and carrot. Wrap in several thicknesses of paper towels; squeeze to remove excess moisture. Place potatoes, carrot, onion, flour, egg, salt and pepper in medium bowl; mix well.

2. Heat oil in large skillet over medium heat. Drop spoonfuls of potato mixture into skillet; flatten to form thin pancakes. Cook 5 minutes or until browned on bottom; turn pancakes and cook 5 minutes or until potatoes are tender.

Makes about 12 pancakes

Roasted Vegetable Omelet with Fresh Salsa ▶

Fresh Salsa (recipe follows)
4 small red-skinned potatoes, scrubbed and quartered
⅓ cup coarsely chopped red bell pepper
2 slices bacon, chopped
1 medium green onion, thinly sliced

3 eggs
Salt and black pepper to taste
1 tablespoon margarine or butter
⅓ cup shredded Colby cheese
Fresh cilantro sprigs for garnish

1. Prepare Fresh Salsa. Preheat oven to 425°F. Grease 15×10-inch jelly-roll pan.

2. Combine potatoes, bell pepper, bacon and green onion in prepared pan. Bake 30 minutes or until potatoes are tender, stirring occasionally.

3. Beat eggs, 1 tablespoon water, salt and black pepper in small bowl. Melt margarine in 10-inch skillet over medium-high heat. Pour egg mixture into skillet; cook until eggs begin to set. Gently lift sides of omelet with spatula to allow liquid to run underneath.

4. When omelet is set but not dry and bottom is lightly browned, remove from heat. Place roasted vegetable mixture over half of omelet; sprinkle with cheese. Gently fold omelet in half. Transfer to serving plate. Serve warm with Fresh Salsa. Garnish, if desired.

Makes 2 servings

Fresh Salsa

3 medium plum tomatoes, seeded and chopped
2 tablespoons chopped onion
1 small jalapeño pepper, seeded and minced*

1 tablespoon chopped fresh cilantro
1 tablespoon lime juice
¼ teaspoon salt
⅛ teaspoon black pepper

Stir together tomatoes, onion, jalapeño pepper, cilantro, lime juice, salt and black pepper. Refrigerate until ready to serve.

*Jalapeño peppers can sting and irritate the skin; wear rubber gloves when handling peppers and do not touch eyes. Wash hands after handling.

Potato Breakfast Custard ▶

3 large Colorado russet variety
    potatoes, peeled and thinly
    sliced
Salt and black pepper
8 ounces low-fat bulk sausage,
    cooked and crumbled*
⅓ cup roasted red pepper, thinly
    sliced *or* 1 jar (2 ounces)
    sliced pimientos, drained

3 eggs
1 cup low-fat milk
3 tablespoons chopped chives or
    green onion tops
¾ teaspoon dried thyme or
    oregano leaves, crushed
Salsa and sour cream
    (optional)

Preheat oven to 375°F. Butter 8- or 9-inch square baking dish or other small casserole. Arrange ½ of potatoes in baking dish. Season to taste with salt and black pepper. Cover with ½ of sausage. Arrange the remaining potatoes over sausage; season to taste with salt and black pepper. Top with remaining sausage and red peppers. Beat eggs, milk, chives and thyme until blended. Pour over potatoes. Cover baking dish with foil and bake 45 to 50 minutes or until potatoes are tender. Uncover and bake 5 to 10 minutes longer. Serve with salsa and sour cream, if desired. *Makes 4 to 5 servings*

*Substitute 6 ounces finely diced lean ham or 6 ounces crumbled, cooked turkey bacon for sausage, if desired.

Nutrients per serving *(¼ of recipe): Calories: 255, Total Fat: 13 g, Cholesterol: 132 mg, Sodium: 431 mg, Protein: 13 g, Dietary Fiber: 2 g*

Favorite recipe from ***Colorado Potato Administrative Committee***

Farmstand Frittata ▶

Nonstick cooking spray
½ cup chopped onion
1 medium red bell pepper, cut
    into thin strips
1 cup cooked quartered
    unpeeled red-skinned
    potatoes
1 cup broccoli florets, blanched
    and drained

6 egg whites
1 cup cholesterol-free egg
    substitute
1 tablespoon chopped fresh
    parsley
½ teaspoon salt
¼ teaspoon black pepper
½ cup (2 ounces) shredded
    reduced-fat Cheddar cheese

1. Spray large nonstick ovenproof skillet with cooking spray; heat over medium heat until hot. Add onion and bell pepper; cook and stir 3 minutes or until crisp-tender. Add potatoes and broccoli; cook and stir 1 to 2 minutes or until heated through.

2. Whisk together egg whites, egg substitute, parsley, salt and black pepper in medium bowl.

3. Spread vegetables in even layer in skillet. Pour egg white mixture over vegetables; cover and cook over medium heat 10 to 12 minutes or until egg mixture is set.

4. Meanwhile, preheat broiler. Top frittata with cheese. Broil, 4 inches from heat, 1 minute or until cheese is bubbly and golden brown. Cut into wedges.

Makes 5 servings

Nutrients per serving: Calories: 143, Total Fat: 2 g, Saturated Fat: 1 g, Cholesterol: 8 mg, Sodium: 459 mg, Protein: 14 g, Dietary Fiber: 3 g

San Juan Quiche

1 sheet frozen puff pastry,
   thawed
3 medium Colorado potatoes,
   thinly sliced
4 slices bacon, cooked and
   drained
1 cup (4 ounces) shredded
   Gruyère cheese

4 eggs, beaten
1 cup light cream or half-and-
   half
½ cup soft bread crumbs
¼ cup shredded Asiago cheese

Preheat oven to 375°F. Roll out pastry sheet to 13-inch round; carefully press pastry onto bottom and up side of quiche dish. Prick bottom of dish with fork. Bake 12 to 15 minutes or until golden brown. Remove from oven.

Meanwhile, place potatoes in medium saucepan. Cover with salted water. Bring to a boil over high heat. Reduce heat to low. Simmer 6 to 8 minutes or until potatoes are just tender; drain. Crumble bacon; spinkle evenly over pastry. Top with potato slices and Gruyère cheese. Combine eggs and cream in medium bowl; pour over potatoes. Combine bread crumbs and Asiago cheese; sprinkle over potato mixture. Bake 30 to 40 minutes or until nearly set in center. Let stand 5 minutes. Cut into wedges.

Makes 6 servings

Nutrients per serving: *Calories: 452, Total Fat: 29 g, Cholesterol: 186 mg, Sodium: 575 mg, Protein: 17 g, Dietary Fiber: 1 g*

Favorite recipe from ***Colorado Potato Administrative Committee***

Sweet Potato Biscuits ▶

2½ cups all-purpose flour
¼ cup packed brown sugar
1 tablespoon baking powder
¾ teaspoon salt
¾ teaspoon ground cinnamon
¼ teaspoon ground ginger

¼ teaspoon ground allspice
½ cup shortening
½ cup chopped pecans
¾ cup mashed canned sweet
   potatoes
½ cup milk

1. Preheat oven to 450°F.

2. Combine flour, sugar, baking powder, salt, cinnamon, ginger and allspice in medium bowl. Cut in shortening with pastry blender or 2 knives until mixture resembles coarse crumbs. Stir in pecans.

3. Combine sweet potatoes and milk in medium bowl with wire whisk until smooth. Make well in center of dry ingredients. Add sweet potato mixture; stir until mixture forms soft dough that clings together and forms a ball.

4. Turn out dough onto well floured surface. Knead dough gently 10 to 12 times. Roll or pat dough to ½-inch thickness. Cut out dough with floured 2½-inch biscuit cutter.

5. Place biscuits 2 inches apart on *ungreased* baking sheet. Bake 12 to 14 minutes or until tops and bottoms are golden brown. Serve warm.   *Makes about 12 biscuits*

Guido's Omelet

1 cup FRANK'S or SNOWFLOSS
    Italian Style Diced Tomatoes,
    drained
12 ounces bulk sausage
1 cup diced potatoes
1 medium onion, chopped

⅓ cup diced green bell pepper
1 tablespoon Worcestershire
    sauce
Butter or nonstick cooking
    spray
6 eggs, beaten

1. Crumble sausage in skillet. Brown over medium-high heat. Drain well.

2. Reduce heat to medium; add tomatoes, potatoes, onion, pepper and Worcestershire sauce. Cook uncovered 3 to 4 minutes. Remove from heat.

3. Coat 10-inch skillet with butter; heat over medium heat. Pour eggs into skillet. Cook until eggs are set on the bottom.

4. Spread sausage mixture evenly over eggs. Cover and cook 2 to 3 minutes or until top is set. Fold omelet in half or thirds. *Makes 2 servings*

Prep Time: 15 minutes   **Cook Time:** 10 minutes

Potato Parmesan Muffins

1 medium Colorado potato,
    peeled and coarsely chopped
Milk
1⅔ cups all-purpose flour
3 to 4 tablespoons grated
    Parmesan cheese, divided
3 tablespoons sugar

2 teaspoons baking powder
½ teaspoon dried basil leaves,
    crushed
¼ teaspoon baking soda
¼ cup vegetable oil
1 egg, beaten

Preheat oven at 400°F. Grease 10 muffin cups or line muffin cups with paper baking cups. Place potato and ½ cup water in small saucepan. Bring to a boil over high heat. Reduce heat to low. Cook, covered, 10 minutes or until tender. (Do not drain.) Mash potato until smooth or place mixture in blender container and blend until smooth. Place in 1-cup measure; add milk to measure 1 cup.

Combine flour, 2 tablespoons Parmesan cheese, sugar, baking powder, basil and soda in large bowl. Combine potato mixture, oil and egg in small bowl; add all at once to flour mixture. Stir just until dry ingredients are moistened. Spoon batter into prepared muffin cups. Sprinkle tops with remaining 1 to 2 tablespoons Parmesan cheese. Bake 20 minutes or until lightly browned. Remove from pan and cool on wire rack.

Makes 10 muffins

Nutrients per serving *(1 muffin): Calories: 170, Total Fat: 7 g, Cholesterol: 23 mg, Sodium: 174 mg, Protein: 4 g, Dietary Fiber: 1 g*

*Favorite recipe of **Colorado Potato Administrative Committee***

Potato and Apple Sauté

2 medium baking potatoes, peeled and diced	1 cup chopped onion
4 strips bacon, diced	1 small, tart green apple, peeled, cored and diced
3 tablespoons olive oil	1 teaspoon sugar
½ cup BLUE DIAMOND® Chopped Natural Almonds	½ teaspoon salt
	1 teaspoon black pepper

Cook potatoes in salted, boiling water until barely tender. Drain and set aside. Sauté bacon in oil in medium skillet over medium heat until soft and translucent. Add almonds; sauté until almonds are crisp. Remove bacon and almonds with slotted spoon to paper towels to drain.

In fat remaining in pan, sauté onion until translucent. Add potatoes and sauté until potatoes and onion begin to brown. Add apple and continue to cook until apple is tender but still hold its shape. Return bacon and almonds to pan. Sprinkle with sugar and salt. Sauté 1 to 2 minutes longer until sugar dissolves. Stir in pepper.

Makes 4 to 6 servings

ACKNOWLEDGMENTS

The publisher would like to thank the companies and organizations listed below for the use of their recipes and photographs in this publication.

American Lamb Council

Bertolli U.S.A., Inc.

Birds Eye

Blue Diamond Growers

California Tomato Commission

Canned Food Information Council

Colorado Potato Administrative Committee

Filippo Berio Olive Oil

Florida Department of Agriculture and Consumer Services,
Bureau of Seafood and Aquaculture

The Fremont Company, Makers of Frank's & SnowFloss Kraut and
Tomato Products

Guiltless Gourmet, Incorporated

Hormel Foods Corporation

Idaho® Potato Commission

Kraft Foods, Inc.

Lawry's® Foods, Inc.

McIlhenny Company

Nabisco, Inc.

National Turkey Federation

Reckitt & Colman Inc.

StarKist® Seafood Company

Wisconsin Milk Marketing Board

INDEX

METRIC CONVERSION CHART

VOLUME MEASUREMENTS (dry)

⅛ teaspoon = 0.5 mL

¼ teaspoon = 1 mL

½ teaspoon = 2 mL

¾ teaspoon = 4 mL

1 teaspoon = 5 mL

1 tablespoon = 15 mL

2 tablespoons = 30 mL

¼ cup = 60 mL

⅓ cup = 75 mL

½ cup = 125 mL

⅔ cup = 150 mL

¾ cup = 175 mL

1 cup = 250 mL

2 cups = 1 pint = 500 mL

3 cups = 750 mL

4 cups = 1 quart = 1 L

VOLUME MEASUREMENTS (fluid)

1 fluid ounce (2 tablespoons) = 30 mL

4 fluid ounces (½ cup) = 125 mL

8 fluid ounces (1 cup) = 250 mL

12 fluid ounces (1½ cups) = 375 mL

16 fluid ounces (2 cups) = 500 mL

WEIGHTS (mass)

½ ounce = 15 g

1 ounce = 30 g

3 ounces = 90 g

4 ounces = 120 g

8 ounces = 225 g

10 ounces = 285 g

12 ounces = 360 g

16 ounces = 1 pound = 450 g

DIMENSIONS

1/16 inch = 2 mm

⅛ inch = 3 mm

¼ inch = 6 mm

½ inch = 1.5 cm

¾ inch = 2 cm

1 inch = 2.5 cm

OVEN TEMPERATURES

250°F = 120°C

275°F = 140°C

300°F = 150°C

325°F = 160°C

350°F = 180°C

375°F = 190°C

400°F = 200°C

425°F = 220°C

450°F = 230°C

BAKING PAN SIZES

Utensil	Size in Inches/ Quarts	Metric Volume	Size in Centimeters
Baking or Cake Pan (square or rectangular)	8×8×2	2 L	20×20×5
	9×9×2	2.5 L	22×22×5
	12×8×2	3 L	30×20×5
	13×9×2	3.5 L	33×23×5
Loaf Pan	8×4×3	1.5 L	20×10×7
	9×5×3	2 L	23×13×7
Round Layer Cake Pan	8×1½	1.2 L	20×4
	9×1½	1.5 L	23×4
Pie Plate	8×1¼	750 mL	20×3
	9×1¼	1 L	23×3
Baking Dish or Casserole	1 quart	1 L	—
	1½ quart	1.5 L	—
	2 quart	2 L	—